AF614913

THE PERSON BEHIND THE BRAND

Written by Annette Whipple

Illustrated by Gary Boller

TABLE OF CONTENTS

A Starfish Book

Teaching Tips for Caregivers:

As a caregiver, you can help your child succeed in school by giving them a strong foundation in language and literacy skills and a desire to learn to read.

This book helps children grow by letting them practice reading skills.

Reading for pleasure and interest will help your child develop reading skills and will give your child the opportunity to practice these skills in meaningful ways.

- Encourage your child to read on their own at home.
- Encourage your child to practice reading aloud.
- Encourage activities that require reading.
- Establish a reading time.
- Talk with your child.
- Give your child writing materials.

Teaching Tips for Teachers:

Research shows that one of the best ways for students to learn a new topic is to read about it.

Before Reading

- Read the "Words to Know" and discuss the meaning of each word.
- Read the back cover to see what the book is about.

During Reading

- When a student gets to a word that is unknown, ask them to look at the rest of the sentence to find clues to help with the meaning of the unknown word.
- Ask the student to write down any pages of the book that were confusing to them.

After Reading

- Discuss the main idea of the book.
- Ask students to give one detail that they learned from the book by showing a text-dependent answer from the book.

OLE KIRK CHRISTIANSEN—LEGO

Ole (OH-lay) Kirk Christiansen invented LEGO building bricks.

It took a long time and a lot of hard work.

Ole was born in the country of Denmark in 1891.

There were 15 people in his family.

Young Ole earned money to help his family.

He took care of sheep and cows.

Ole learned how to make things from wood.

He bought a **carpentry** shop.

He built houses, barns, and furniture.

A fire destroyed Ole's workshop and home.

Ole just built them again.

He made more **products** in his new workshop.

Many people were poor during the **Great Depression**.

They did not have money to buy big things.

Ole began to make smaller things like toys.

Soon, Ole was making only wooden toys.

He named his toy shop LEGO.

LEGO comes from Danish words that mean "play well."

Another fire burned down the toy **factory**.

Ole did not give up.

He just built it again.

Ole wanted to try something new.

He made building bricks from **plastic** instead of wood.

The plastic bricks were very popular.

Kids and adults loved LEGO sets.

They could combine sets.

They could build something new each time they played.

21

After Ole died, his family kept the LEGO **business**.

They still own LEGO.

About seven LEGO sets are sold every second!

OLE KIRK CHRISTIANSEN

in 1957

People around the world can build with LEGO because Ole never gave up.

Words to Know

business (BIZ-nis): an organization that makes and sells products or services

carpentry (KAHR-puhn-tree): building and repairing items made from wood

factory (FAK-tur-ee): a building where products such as toys are made in large numbers

Great Depression (grate di-PRESH-uhn): a time from 1929 to 1939 when many people did not have a lot of money

plastic (PLAS-tik): a light, strong, man-made substance that can be molded into different shapes

products (PRAH-duhkts): items made to be sold

Index

Comprehension Questions

1. Ole Kirk Christiansen was born in ________.

a. Denmark
b. Norway
c. Canada

2. Ole bought a ______.

a. newspaper business
b. carpentry shop
c. candy store

3. Ole rebuilt after a fire ________.

a. one time
b. two times
c. three times

4. True or false: Ole grew up in a small family.

5. True or false: LEGO bricks are made from plastic.

Answers:
1. a, 2. b, 3. b, 4. False, 5. True

About the Author

Annette Whipple celebrates curiosity through her books. She wrote *The Laura Ingalls Wilder Companion*, *Whooo Knew? The Truth About Owls*, and *Quirky Critter Devotions*. She lives with her family in Pennsylvania where she appreciates the natural beauty around her. Get to know Annette at www.AnnetteWhipple.com.

About the Illustrator

Gary Boller lives in the glorious countryside in Hampshire, UK, with his wife and two children, one Chihuahua, and four cats. He always doodled as a kid, even on his parents' walls, and loved the comics of the day. Gary also loves music and has played double bass in bands. He has toured all over Europe many times and the USA twice. He's currently learning fiddle, much to the annoyance of his pets.

Written by: Annette Whipple
Illustrated by: Gary Boller
Designed by: Under the Oaks
Editor: Kim Thompson
Production manager:
Candice Campbell

Library of Congress PCN Data
Ole Kirk Christiansen / Annette Whipple
The Person Behind the Brand
ISBN 979-8-8945-9119-3 (hard cover)
ISBN 979-8-8945-9124-7 (paperback)
ISBN 979-8-8945-9134-6 (EPUB)
ISBN 979-8-8945-9129-2 (eBook)
Library of Congress Control Number:
2024946246

Seahorse Publishing Company
www.seahorsepub.com

Printed in the U.S.A./CP112025

Published in the United States
Seahorse Publishing
PO Box 771325
Coral Springs, FL 33077